Like our Facebook page
@RiddlesandGiggles

Follow us on Instagram
@RiddlesandGiggles_Official

Questions & Customer Service
hello@riddlesandgiggles.com

Christmas Joke Book for Kic

by Riddles and Giggles™

www.riddlesandgiggles.com

D1276774

FREE BONUS

Get your FREE book download

*Christmas Jokes & Would You
Rather for Kids*

- ⊘ Contains a collection of cracking
  Christmas jokes and Would You Rather
  Christmas-themed questions

- ⊘ More endless giggles and
  entertainment for the whole family.

**Claim your FREE book at
www.riddlesandagiggles.com/christmas**

Or scan with your phone to
get your free download

TABLE OF CONTENTS

WELCOME

Hi there, Jokester!

Jokes are a great way for people to have fun and share laughs together.

Lots of people love to tell jokes. Some are very funny. Some are just corny. Other jokes make no sense at all. One thing we can agree on about jokes is that kids love them!

I hope you are one of those kids because if you want a collection of funny, corny, and laugh-out-loud jokes, this book is for you!

The *Christmas Joke Book for Kids* is an excellent collection of good, clean, fun jokes that will make you roll your eyes, snort, giggle, groan, and laugh out loud.

You can read this whole book or pick which jokes you want to read in any order you want.

You can also enjoy reading the jokes on your own or share the jokes with everyone around you. Or you can take turns reading the jokes out loud with family and friends.

PSST… You can also color the Christmas pictures to use this book as a coloring book AND a joke book!

Fun Ideas for Christmas Day

Before we get to the jokes, here are a few ways you can add some giggles and laughs to your Christmas celebrations.

Make joke napkin rings! Cut strips of paper (about 2 inches x 5 inches) and write jokes on them. Tape the ends together and use them as napkin rings. You can get creative and use colored paper and stickers or draw some decorations.

Make place cards! Take a piece of cardstock and cut it in half. Fold each piece in half again. Write the name of each guest on one side and a joke or two on the other.

Give a performance! Ask your siblings or guests to join you and then entertain the crowd. Take turns reading joke questions out loud and have the others answer the joke.

Team activity! Create two teams. Give each team a list of different jokes. Teams go back and forth telling jokes and get a point for every joke they're able to correctly answer. The team with the most points wins something.

....

Tips on How to Tell a Joke

- Practice reading the joke out loud a few times to help you remember it. You may want to practice reading in front of a mirror.

- Find a family member or friend and ask them if they want to hear a joke.

- As you tell the joke, remember to say it slowly and clearly so people understand every word.

- Adding a small pause helps to build up suspense and can make the joke even funnier.

- Deliver the final punch line. Remember to say it slowly, then wait for the laughs.

- If you mess up, that's OK. Move on and tell another joke. Remember, everyone loves jokes!

1

SANTA AND HIS HELPERS

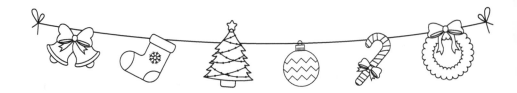

How does Santa like to celebrate when the elves finish making all the toys?

He gives them a round of Santa-plause.

What are Santa's favorite snack foods?

Ho Hos and Crisp Pringles.

At the North Pole, what do police elves enforce?

Santa Laws.

What did Santa say when he crashed his sleigh?

"Well, now I'm really Scrooged!"

What song do the elves always sing for Santa on his birthday?

"Freeze a Jolly Good Fellow."

What reindeer game do reindeer play at sleepovers?

Truth or Deer.

How many chimneys does Santa go down?

Stacks.

Why did the elf win the argument about his ears?

He had some good points.

What color looks best
on Santa Claus?

Red, because it suits him.

What do you get when
you cross Santa Claus
with a great white shark?

Santa Jaws.

What do you call
a reindeer with
poor manners?

Rude-olph.

What device does Santa
use to snap photos
at his workshop?

A polar-oid camera.

How does Rudolph
count down the days
until Christmas?

*He uses an advent
calen-deer.*

What do you call a
reindeer with no eyes?

No idea.

What do you call
a reindeer with no
eyes AND no legs?

Still no idea.

What do you call a
reindeer that has
one eye and lends
a helping hand?

A good eye-deer.

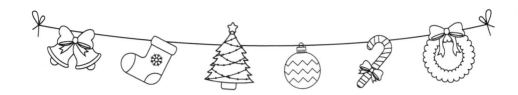

Where does Santa stay when he goes on a holiday?

At a ho, ho, hotel.

What does Santa say to the elves when they eat all the Christmas treats?

"Don't be elf-ish!"

Why doesn't Santa get sick from all the chimney soot?

He gets a flue shot.

Which one of Santa's reindeer has the best moves?

Dancer.

How do you know that Santa is an expert at karate?

He has a black belt.

What did Rudolph say to Santa when he guided them through the blizzard?

"Hold on for deer life!"

What did the elves tell Mrs. Claus when she wore her new Christmas dress?

"Sleigh queen, sleigh!"

What dish do the elves order at the North Pole Restaurant?

Elf-abet soup.

What do you get when you cross Santa with a flying saucer?

A U-F-HO-HO-HO.

What does Santa say when the elves tell him something surprising?

"Sleigh-what!?"

SANTA AND HIS HELPERS

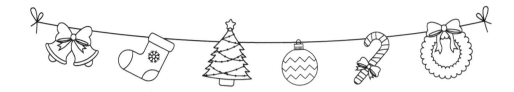

What do you call
an elf cowboy?

A jolly rancher.

Which subject at school did
Santa excel at the most?

Chemis-tree.

What does Rudolph
want for Christmas?

A Pony sleigh station.

What kind of books
does Santa recommend
to his elves?

Elf-help books.

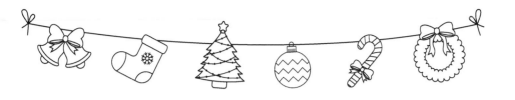

What do you call a Santa from the South Pole?

A lost claus.

What do you call a reindeer with three eyes?

A reiiindeer.

Why don't elves from the North Pole get along with elves from the South Pole?

They're Pole-ar opposites.

Why do elves make good listeners?

Because they're all ears.

What is the name of Santa's pet dog?

Santa Paws.

Why is Santa afraid of getting stuck in a chimney?

Because he has claus-trophobia.

What kind of bike does
Santa Claus ride?

A Holly Davidson.

What do you call Santa
when he's taking a break?

Santa Pause.

What is Santa's
favorite drink?

Beer-d.

What kind of photographs
do elves like taking?

Elfies.

How much did Santa pay for his sleigh?

Nothing, his sleigh was on the house.

Why doesn't Santa need to put his elves through training?

They're elf-taught.

What does Santa use to measure?

Santameters.

How do elves greet each other?

"Small world, isn't it?"

What does Santa use every time he finishes delivering presents to stop the spread of germs from house to house?

Santa-tizer.

Which one of Santa's reindeer is the cleanest?

Comet.

What is an elf's favorite sport?

Miniature golf.

What do elves answer when Santa takes a roll call?

"PRESENT!"

Why did Santa get a parking ticket?

He left his sleigh in a snow parking zone.

What's red, white, and falls down chimneys?

Santa Klutz.

What does Santa use when he goes fishing?

His North Pole.

Which singer do reindeer like to listen to?

Beyon-sleigh.

SANTA AND HIS HELPERS

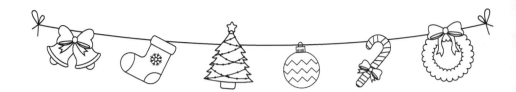

Where does Santa go
to learn how to slide
down chimneys?

A chimnasium.

Why do reindeer tell
the best stories?

*They always carry a
tail with them.*

What do elves do
after school?

Their gnome-work.

What do you call Santa
when he's lost his pants?

Saint Knickerless.

Why did Santa put a
clock in his sleigh?

*Because he wanted
to see time fly.*

Where do Santa and
his elves go to vote?

The North Poll.

Why did the reindeer
cross the road?

To deliver presents.

What does Santa
do when his elves
misbehave?

He gives them the sack.

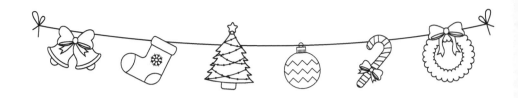

Why did no one bid for Rudolph and Blitzen on eBay?

Because they were two deer.

What do reindeer say before they tell you a joke?

"This one's gonna sleigh you!"

What's Santa's favorite sandwich?

Peanut butter and jolly.

How do you know when Santa's around?

You can always sense his presents.

Where does Santa store
his suit after Christmas?

In the Claus-et.

Why does Santa
love to golf?

*He always gets a HO-
HO-Hole in one.*

What game do
Santa's reindeer play
in their stalls?

Stable tennis.

Who looks after Santa
when he gets ill?

The National Elf Service.

2

CHRISTMAS TREES & DECORATIONS

What do you call
edible Christmas
tree decorations?

Orna-mints.

Why do Christmas trees
make great doctors?

*They are good
with needles.*

What do Christmas trees
say before the Christmas
lights are switched on?

*"On your marks,
get set... glow!"*

How do you compliment
a Christmas tree?

*By telling them they
look tree-mendous.*

What do you call a Christmas tree that likes to spy on its neighbors?

A nosey bark-er.

How did the two rival Christmas trees get along?

They signed a peace tree-ty.

What did the bauble ask his best friend?

"Do you want to hang later?"

Why are Christmas decorations bad at talking on the phone?

They are always hanging up.

What did the Christmas tree say to the string of lights?

"You truly light up my world."

What do you call three Christmas trees standing together?

A tree-o.

Why are Christmas trees
always so well-rested?

They sleep like logs.

How do Christmas angels
greet each other?

"Halo."

What did the dog say
to the Christmas tree?

*"My bark is way
louder than yours."*

What do you call a
Christmas tree you
forget to water?

Nevergreen.

What did one Christmas
tree say to the other one
that was feeling down?

*"Lighten up. It's almost
Christmas time!"*

Why did nobody want
to hang out with the
Elf on the Shelf?

*He was acting way
too shelf-ish.*

What do you call
wrapping paper left over
from opening presents?

Christmess.

Where do young
saplings learn to become
Christmas trees?

In elemen-tree school.

What happens if you eat
Christmas decorations?

You get tinsel-itis.

What did the
Christmas tree say
to the ornament?

*"Aren't you tired of
hanging around?"*

How do fish celebrate Christmas?

They hang reefs on the door.

What did the Christmas tree
say to the light bulb?

"Hey! Just had a bright idea!"

How did the ornament get
addicted to Christmas?

He was hooked on trees his whole life.

What happens when you give a
Christmas tree a present?

It lights up.

What dessert do Christmas trees love?

Tree-cle tart.

3

CHRISTMAS FESTIVITIES

What are the best
Christmas sweaters
made from?

Fleece Navidad.

Why don't kids like eating
broken candy canes?

*They prefer ones that
are in mint condition.*

What did Adam say the
day before Christmas?

"It's Christmas, Eve!"

Which dinosaur loves
Christmas the most?

A Tree-Rex

When do gingerbread men
get to take a sick day?

*When they are
feeling crummy.*

What do fish sing
at Christmas?

Christmas corals.

How do snow globes feel
around Christmas time?

A little shaken.

Why does a broken
drum make a great
Christmas gift?

You just can't beat it.

What should you tell yourself if you are having trouble wrapping a present?

"Never gift up."

Why don't lobsters give presents at Christmas?

Because they're shell-fish.

What do frogs say on Christmas day when they are opening their presents.

"Rippit, rippit, just rippit!"

What did the bald man say when he got a comb for Christmas?

"Thanks, I'll never part with it."

What did Frosty say when he received his many Christmas gifts?

"Thank you all snow much."

What did the Christmas stocking say when it had a hole in it?

"Well, I'll be darned!"

What's the difference between the Christmas alphabet and the ordinary alphabet?

The Christmas alphabet has NOEL in it.

Which insect dislikes Christmas?

A humbug.

What's the best-selling breakfast cereal in the North Pole?

Frosted Flakes.

Which Christmas vegetables are
always dripping with water?

Leeks and the Brussels spouts.

Why did the Grinch go to the liquor store?

He was searching for some holiday spirit.

What's the best thing to give your parents for Christmas?

A list of everything you want.

When does Christmas come before Thanksgiving?

In the dictionary.

What do you call a person who steals
secret Christmas recipes?

A secret mince-spy.

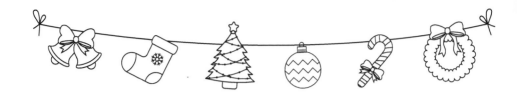

What should you do
if your car stalls on
Christmas Eve?

You get a mistletow.

Where do werewolves
buy Christmas gifts?

Beast Buy.

What do you get from a
cow in the North Pole?

Ice cream.

How does Ebenezer
Scrooge get drunk?

On Christmas spirits.

What did the
peppermint bark say
to the candy cane?

*"Looks like we're mint
for each other."*

What did the peanut
butter say to the
grape on Christmas?

*"'Tis the season
to be jelly!"*

Why couldn't the
toys fall asleep on
Christmas night?

They were all wound up.

Which Christmas carol
is a parent's favorite?

Silent Night.

What song do mite
insects listen to
at Christmas?

Fleas Navidad.

What do sheep say to
each other at Christmas?

"Season's bleatings!"

Which vegetable at
Christmas dinner is
the best at giving
a haircut?

Parsnips.

What is a
vegan's favorite
Christmas carol?

Soy to the World.

Why does Scrooge love
reindeer so much?

*Because every single
buck is dear to him.*

CHRISTMAS JOKE BOOK FOR KIDS

How do you help someone who's lost their Christmas spirit?

Nurse them back to elf.

Why is a foot a good Christmas present?

It makes for a good stocking stuffer.

What did the stamp say to the Christmas card?

Stick with me and we'll go places.

WINTER FUN

What falls but never
hurts itself?

Snow.

What does Jack Frost
like best about school?

Snow and tell.

While sniffing the air, what
did one snowman say to
the other snowman?

*"Is it just me, or do
you smell carrots?"*

What is it called when
a snowman has an
emotional outburst?

A meltdown.

Why was the penguin afraid to jump off the iceberg?

He was scared of heights and got cold feet.

How does a penguin fix a broken house?

Igloos it back together.

Why did Humpty Dumpty have a miserable winter?

Because he had a great fall.

What do you call a snowman who lives in a remote area?

Ice-olated.

What game do snowmen
play with their chill-dren?

Ice-spy with My Little Eye.

How do snowmen
like to travel?

*They prefer to ride
their b-icicles.*

What did the police shout
to the snowman when
they caught him stealing?

"Freeze!"

What does a book
do in the winter?

Puts on a jacket.

What do you get
when you mix Count
Dracula with Frosty?

Frost-bite.

Why is Christmas the coldest holiday?

It's always in Decem-brrr.

How do snowmen greet each other?

"It's ICE to meet you."

How do snowmen say goodbye to each other?

"Have an ICE day!"

What is a snowman's favorite movie?

The Blizzard of Oz.

What did the polar bear say to the barista?

"Can you please paw me an iced coffee?"

What do snowmen like to put on their sandwiches?

Cold cuts.

What does Jack Frost become when he is super annoyed?

Very frost-rated.

What did the snowflake say to the sidewalk?

"Let's stick together."

How do fireplaces feel when winter is approaching?

They get really stoked.

What do you get when you cross a snowman with a baker?

Frosty the Dough-man.

What did the snowman's hat say to the scarf?

You hang around while I go on a head.

Who is Jack Frost's favorite aunt?

Aunt Arctica.

What happened when the icicle fell on the snowman's head?

It knocked him out cold.

What do you call a dog in the winter?

A chilly dog.

Where do snowmen go to dance?

Snowballs.

What do you call an old snowman?

Water.

What's a snowman's favorite food?

Brrrrrr-itos.

Why does everyone love Jack Frost?

Because he's cool.

What's a snowman's favorite snack?

Ice Krispy treats.

What did the snowflake say to the fallen leaf?

"You're so last season."

What's the most
competitive season?

Win-ter.

How do you find Will
Smith in the snow?

Follow the fresh prints.

What do snowmen
call their parents?

Mom and Pop-sicle.

What do snowmen take
when they get sick?

A chill pill.

How do you scare
a snowman?

With a hairdryer.

What do snowmen order
at fast-food restaurants?

*An ice burger with
chilly sauce.*

What do you call a
carrotless snowman?

*I'm not sure.
Nobody nose.*

Why do hockey
players never tell
jokes in the rink?

*They're afraid of
cracking up the ice.*

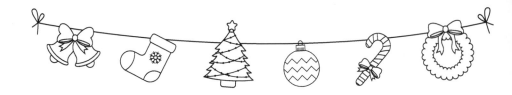

What athlete is warmest in winter?

A long jumper.

What do snowmen like to do on the weekend?

Chill out.

How does a snowman lose weight?

He waits for the weather to get warmer.

Why did the snowman turn yellow?

Ask the dog over there.

Why did the snowman call his dog Frost?

Because Frost bites.

5

PUNS & ONE-LINERS

Sleigh my name,
sleigh my name.

With family and friends
gathered around, I'm
feeling a little extra
Santa-mental.

I'm a rebel without
a Claus.

Have snow fear—
Christmas is here!

Sleigh, what?!
Sleigh it isn't so!

You don't like these
puns? There's myrrh.

You snow the drill.

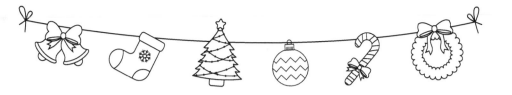

I hate to have the last
laugh, but I told you snow.

Treat yo' elf.

It takes one to snow one.

It's the season of giving.
Don't be elfish.

Icy what you did there.

Have your elf a merry
little Christmas.

This is snow
laughing matter!

Having everyone together brings reindeers to my eyes.

There really is snow place like home.

You've got this. Believe in your elf.

I've been pining to see you all year!

Those Christmas tree decorations look treemendous!

Did you hear about the group of reindeer who got into trouble? Yeah, I herd.

Santa Claus is a
gifted man.

Will Santa launch an
online store? He's
toying with the idea.

I have a special ability
to predict what's
inside a wrapped
present. It's a gift.

Don't like my holiday
puns? That's a little
Rude-olph of you.

Did you hear about the
cracker's Christmas
party? It was a BANG!

Who did all this
Christmas shopping?
Me, my elf, and I!

I love when candy canes
are in mint condition.

Those are some high
quali-tree decorations!

I told you snow.

Yule miss me when
I'm gone!

I'm snow bored.

Don't reindeer on my
Christmas parade.

CHRISTMAS JOKE BOOK FOR KIDS

MERRY CHRISTMAS!

BEFORE YOU GO

Did you have fun with these sometimes-corny Christmas and winter jokes?

Now that you have gotten the hang of jokes, spend some time thinking up some of your own! Create your own jokes about fun things you like about Christmas.

You can create jokes about Santa, Santa's elves and his reindeer, Christmas trees and decorations, Christmas stockings and presents, and traditions you enjoy on Christmas day.

Once you think up your own jokes, you can play the game anywhere! It is a great game to play on long road trips, at school, or even when you are waiting in line at the grocery store.

Have fun coming up with your own jokes and endless giggles!

WRITE YOUR OWN JOKES!

Have fun coming up with your own jokes and endless giggles!

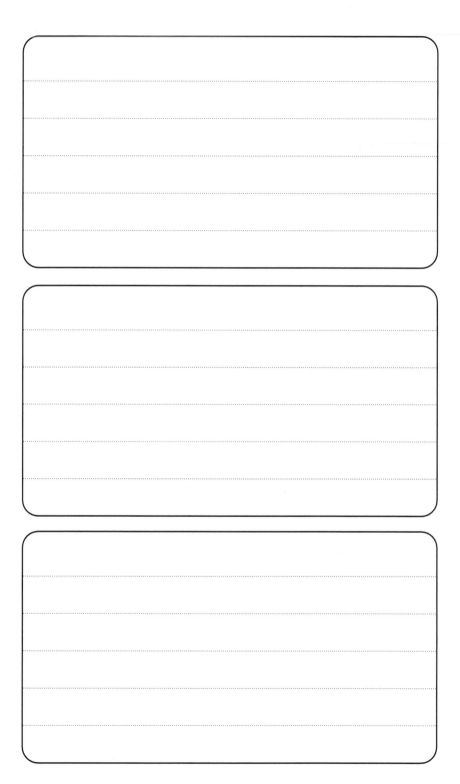

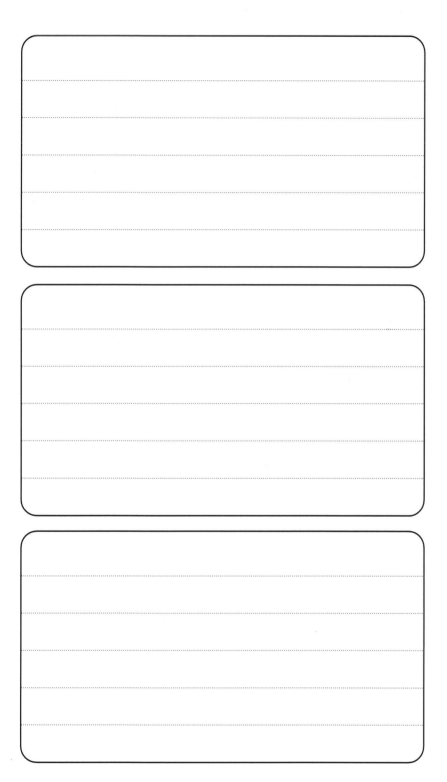

CHRISTMAS JOKE BOOK FOR KIDS

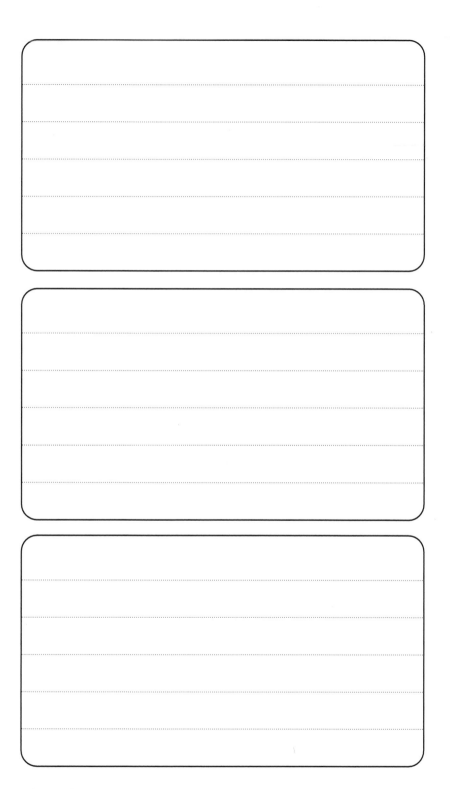

CHRISTMAS JOKE BOOK FOR KIDS

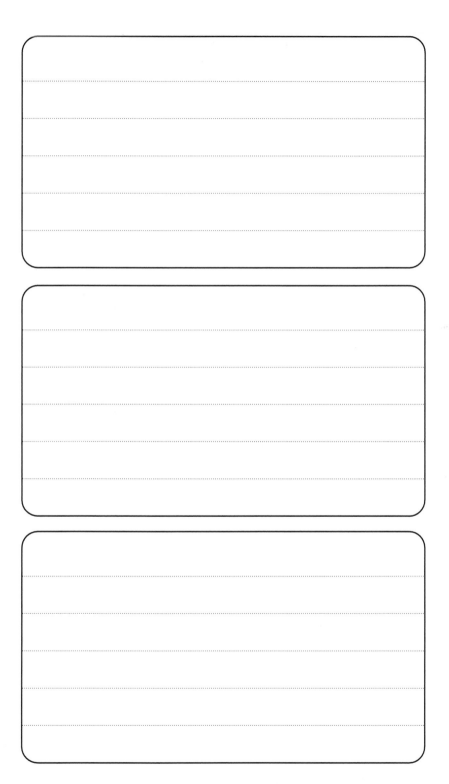

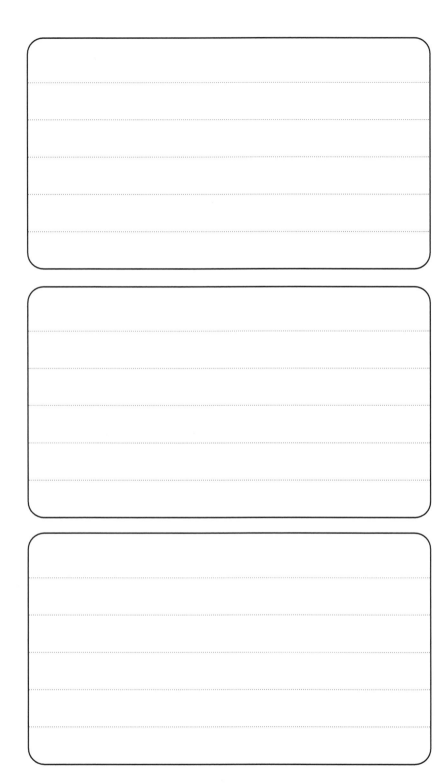

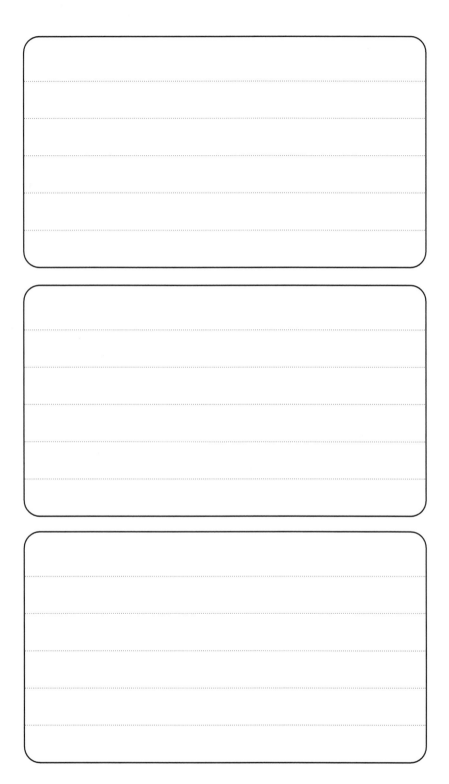

CHRISTMAS JOKE BOOK FOR KIDS

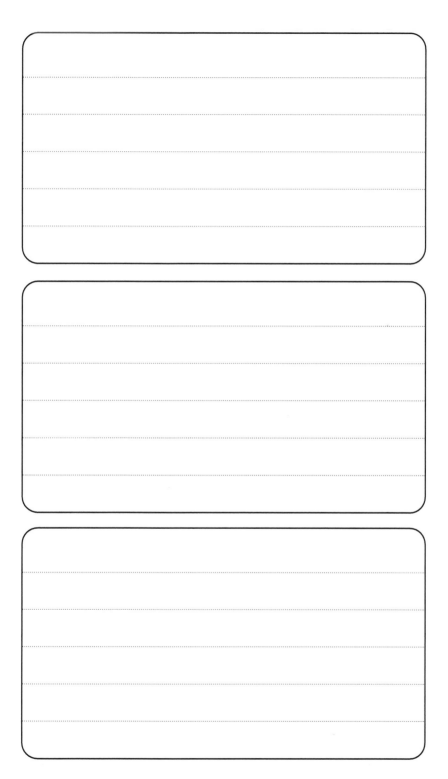

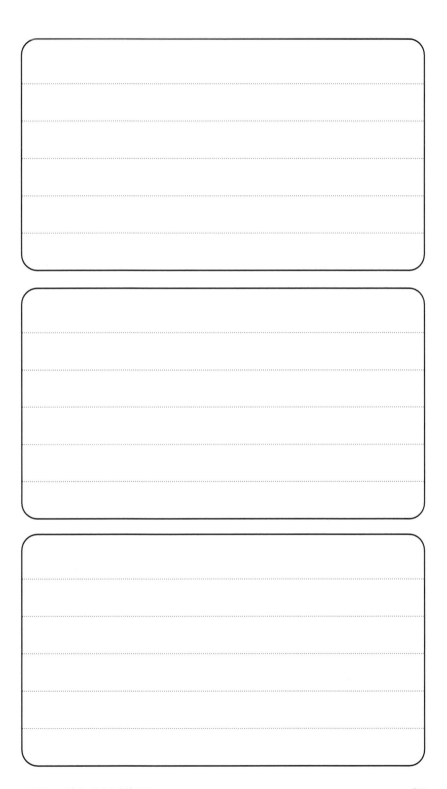

CHRISTMAS JOKE BOOK FOR KIDS

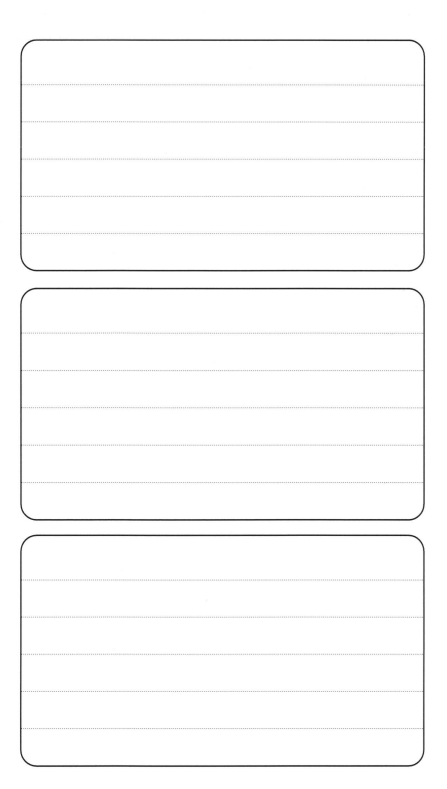

COLLECT THEM ALL!

Christmas
Would You
Rather for Kids

Christmas
Joke Book
for Kids

Christmas
Knock Knock Joke
Book for Kids

www.riddlesandgiggles.com

REFERENCES

20 Clever Winter and Snow Puns for Your Instagram Captions. (2018, December 6). It's Me, JD. https://itsmejd.com/clever-winter-snow-puns-instagram-captions/

24 Wreath Puns - Punstoppable. (n.d.). Punstoppable.com. https://punstoppable.com/Wreath-puns

100 Christmas Jokes and Puns That Are Snow Much Fun. (2021, August 16). Southern Living. https://www.southernliving.com/christmas/christmas-puns-jokes

150+ Fa-La-La-Fantastic Christmas Puns That Will Sleigh The Competition. (2019, October 3). The Right Wording. https://therightwording.com/best-christmas-puns-that-will-sleigh-the-competition/

Chapman, R. (2017, December 16). 42 Santa Puns for Instagram That Will Have You Ho-Ho-Ho-ing With Laughter. Elite Daily. https://www.elitedaily.com/p/42-santa-puns-for-instagram-that-will-have-you-ho-ho-ho-ing-with-laughter-7615791

Chapman, R. (2019, December 19). 28 Xmas Gift Puns That'll Complete Your Post With a Big Red Bow. Elite Daily. https://www.elitedaily.com/p/28-gift-puns-for-christmas-thatll-complete-your-post-with-a-big-red-bow-19492701

Christmas Jokes: Share Our Funny Christmas Jokes. (n.d.). Reader's Digest. https://www.rd.com/jokes/christmas-jokes/

Community, S. (2019, August 1). 80+ Funny Christmas Card Puns for the Holidays | Shutterfly. Ideas & Inspiration. https://www.shutterfly.com/ideas/christmas-card-puns/

Frost, M. (2020). 50 Snow Puns That Are Snow Funny by Kidadl. Kidadl.com. https://kidadl.com/articles/snow-puns-that-are-snow-funny

Green, A. (2020, August 5). 101 Best Snow & Winter Puns for Wintry Instagram Captions. Eternal Arrival. https://eternalarrival.com/quotes/snow-winter-puns-instagram-captions/

John, L. (2021, September 14). 30+ Ice Puns That Won't Slip Your Mind by Kidadl. Kidadl.com. https://kidadl.com/articles/ice-puns-that-wont-slip-your-mind

Mommy, T. S. (2019, October 3). 100+ Scrumptious Food Puns That'll Have You Working up an Appetite. Scary Mommy. https://www.scarymommy.com/food-puns/

Snowflake Puns. (2019, March 3). Punpedia. https://punpedia.org/snowflake-puns/

Stocking. (n.d.). Punpedia. https://punpedia.org/tag/stocking/

White, M. (n.d.). 100+ Christmas Puns So Funny You'll Be Beside Your Elf. Yourdictionary. https://examples.yourdictionary.com/100-christmas-puns-so-funny-youll-be-beside-your-elf.html

Winter. (n.d.). Punpedia. https://punpedia.org/tag/winter/

Made in the USA
Las Vegas, NV
02 December 2021